★ ★ ★

HH-60 PAVE HAWK HELICOPTERS

BY JACK DAVID

BELLWETHER MEDIA · MINNEAPOLIS

Are you ready to take it to the extreme?
Torque books thrust you into the action-packed
world of sports, vehicles, and adventure. These books
may include dirt, smoke, fire, and dangerous stunts.
WARNING: read at your own risk.

Library of Congress Cataloging-in-Publication Data

David, Jack, 1968-
  HH-60 Pave Hawk helicopters / by Jack David.
     p. cm. – (Torque: military machines)
  Includes bibliographical references and index.
  Summary: "Amazing photography and engaging information explain the technologies and
capabilities of the HH-60 Pave Hawk Helicopters. Intended for students in grades 3 through
7"–Provided by publisher.
  ISBN-13: 978-1-60014-223-9 (hardcover : alk. paper)
  ISBN-10: 1-60014-223-0 (hardcover : alk. paper)
  1. Pave Hawk (Search and rescue helicopter)–Juvenile literature. I. Title.

  UG1232.S43D39 2008
  623.74'66–dc22   2008019868

This edition first published in 2009 by Bellwether Media.

The photographs in this book are reproduced through the courtesy of the United States Department of
Defense.

Printed in the United States of America.

CONTENTS

THE HH-60 PAVE HAWK IN ACTION

A hard rain falls from the night sky. A downed United States pilot hides behind enemy lines. He knows enemy soldiers are searching for him. He hears their voices as they approach.

The sound of helicopter blades fills the air. It's a United States Air Force HH-60 Pave Hawk.

⭐ ⭐ ⭐ 5

The helicopter's machine guns rattle as its crew drives back the enemy soldiers. The Pave Hawk dips close to the ground and lowers a rope to the downed pilot. He jumps onto it and climbs into the helicopter. The Pave Hawk rises into the sky. Its **mission** is complete.

RESCUE CHOPPER

The HH-60 Pave Hawk is an Air Force helicopter built for combat search and rescue (CSAR). It is based on the design of the Army's UH-60 Black Hawk. The Black Hawk is a powerful attack helicopter. The Air Force changed the Black Hawk's design to make a helicopter that would be better suited for rescue missions. The Air Force needs the Pave Hawk to rescue pilots that have crashed behind enemy lines.

★ ★ ★

In peacetime, the military uses Pave Hawks to help disaster victims.

Pave Hawks are perfect helicopters for rescue. They are fast and easy to maneuver. They have enough weapons to defend themselves from attack. These features also make them ideal for another mission—they can **insert** Special Forces behind enemy lines.

WEAPONS AND FEATURES

The Pave Hawk has some special features that help with rescues. Its **hoist** can lift 600 pounds (272 kilograms). **Night-vision goggles** and a **forward-looking infrared (FLIR)** system help crews find downed pilots at night and in bad weather. Advanced weather **radar** and communications systems give the crew up-to-date information. Global Positioning System (GPS) equipment helps crews know exactly where they are at all times.

Pave Hawks can be refueled by tanker airplanes while still in flight.

Pave Hawks need weapons to defend themselves and the pilots they rescue. Machine guns are mounted to the sides. Some Pave Hawks have two 7.52-mm **miniguns** instead of machine guns. They can fire thousands of bullets per minute.

★ FAST FACT ★

The rotor blades on a Pave Hawk can be folded
to make the helicopter easier to store.

HH-60 SPECIFICATIONS:

Primary Function: Combat search and rescue (CSAR)

Length: 64 feet, 8 inches (17.1 meters)

Height: 16 feet, 8 inches (4.4 meters)

Weight: 22,000 pounds (9,900 kilograms)

Rotor Diameter: 53 feet, 7 inches (14.1 meters)

Speed: 184 miles (296 kilometers) per hour

Range: 580 miles (940 kilometers)

HH-60 MISSIONS

The main Pave Hawk mission is combat search and rescue. Crews work together to find and rescue crashed pilots. The Pave Hawk's pilot and copilot fly the helicopter. The **gunner** operates the weapons. The **flight engineer** operates the helicopter's many electronic systems. A Pave Hawk may also carry **parajumpers** who can jump to the ground to help injured soldiers.

★ FAST FACT ★

A Pave Hawk's hoist can lower more than 200 feet (61 meters) to get a victim.

A Pave Hawk crew can rescue a victim in several ways. The pilot can land the helicopter and bring the victim on board. The crew can also use the hoist to lower a basket to the person in need of rescue. Ropes or rope ladders are another way to bring a person aboard. Pave Hawk crews will use any method they need to bring soldiers home safely.

GLOSSARY

flight engineer—the crew member who operates a Pave Hawk's electronic equipment

forward-looking infrared (FLIR)—electronic equipment that can detect sources of heat

gunner—the crew member who operates a Pave Hawk's weapons

hoist—a tool on a Pave Hawk that can lower and raise to rescue people

insert—to place a soldier or group of soldiers into enemy territory

minigun—an automatic weapon that can fire thousands of bullets per minute

mission—a military task

night-vision goggles—electronic equipment that helps Pave Hawk pilots see in the dark

parajumper—a soldier who parachutes out of aircraft to fight or to help with a rescue

radar—a sensor system that uses radio waves to locate objects

TO LEARN MORE

AT THE LIBRARY

Holden, Henry M. *Rescue Helicopters and Aircraft.* Berkeley Heights, N.J.: Enslow, 2002.

Stone, Lynn M. *HH-60 Pave Hawk.* Vero beach, Fla.: Rourke, 2004.

Zobel, Derek. *United States Air Force.* Minneapolis, Minn.: Bellwether, 2008.

ON THE WEB

Learning more about military machines is as easy as 1, 2, 3.

1. Go to www.factsurfer.com

2. Enter "military machines" into search box.

3. Click the "Surf" button and you will see a list of related web sites.

With factsurfer.com, finding more information is just a click away.

INDEX